FU
FOR FEMALES

Rib Tickling Rhymes for Women

By
Ellie Kelly

FUNNY FOR FEMALES

Rib Tickling Rhymes for Women

First published in 2017

Cover picture and illustrations
courtesy of Pixabay. com

ISBN - 978-1981268702

Introduction

This book explores some of life's irritations
and that includes men and their limitations.
These poems cut through like a carving knife,
to the the funnier and naughtier side of life.
But please, come on, let me know if you can,
is there anything at all more vexing than man!
You live with his emissions and spurious secretions
while his world revolves around his nether regions!
You will recognise shades of the following traits
that sharing your life with a man incorporates.
So just hold on tight and shout "You're right."
each time a tint of his nuances comes to light.
From the dawn of time men have had to 'bond'
or just used that excuse to escape and abscond.
Swanning off on those 'men only' hunting trips
while we stayed at home and cooked the chips!
Has anything even evolved in his caveman head?
He now goes on stag nights and his cave is a shed!
So read on to find just how far man has come,
it's not actually that far, he still needs his Mum!

Contents

A Self Portrait

I think it's fine and dandy
to keep a man handy,
to do things I'm not good at doing.
But my man also fails
with hammer and nails
but I find he's better at screwing!

Ellie Kelly

Words a Man Should Know

When a woman says, *"Oh, its nothing."*
Then all men should be beware.
"Oh, its nothing," means 'there's something,'
that is festering away in there.

"It's okay," is a phrase roughly the same,
so it will be a chance men take.
We're actually thinking long and hard
on how you'll pay for this mistake.

"Oh please yourself," it sounds so innocent
but it is actually cloaked in stealth.
It means the next time he's expecting nookie
he'll have to literally *'Please himself.'*

"Fine." is a word that we women will use
to end a disagreement or a row.
It means we know that we're in the right
and men should really shut up *'now.'*

Then there comes, "Just do what you want."
Now this is one notch up from "Fine."
This is now their very last warning,
You do not cross this line!

Then along comes the phrase, "Go ahead."
This is a dare and not permission.
It really is a stupid man's last chance
to reverse his last decision.

And then when we say, "We need to talk,"
it states an apology is now needed.
It means that all the warning words before,
have not been noted or heeded!

And finally comes....... "It's too late now."
This will fill him with a chill.
It's used whenever he says he's sorry
and means we're going in for the kill!

Mammograms

Just who was it who invented the mammogram test?
An instrument of torture that clamps to your breast.
Now it must have been a man who came up with that;
a machine that tries to squash an orbicular thing flat!

It's like a leftover device from the Spanish Inquisition,
where torturing good people was a proud tradition.
It's quite unpleasant, it hurts and it's not very nice.
So why don't men have to put their nuts in a vice?

Oh no, compared to us, their knacker test is a dream,
a gentle ultra sound fondle with a soothing gel cream.
Now I bet it was a man who devised a test like that,
a test that makes them all smile like a Cheshire Cat!

Tim once had that test and returned rather subdued.
He said everything was okay but had a peculiar mood.
Then he told me that a woman had conducted the scan
and was it sexist to think it should be done by a man?

I was shocked as he still refers to a woman as a 'bird.'
and I'm sure he thinks a 'sexism' is a four letter word.
I said "If a man did the scan, what if the guy was gay?"
He said "Then there'd be no problem like earlier today."

Then he confided that he'd started getting 'turned on'
and had had to think of **me** until the feeling was gone!
"What the hell do you mean!" I turned round and said,
"I didn't mean it like *that*," he said turning bright red.

"I meant when you're nagging me and giving me grief."
Then he saw the look in my eyes and began to retreat.
He was either lucky that day or must have just guessed,
that his balls were about to get a mammogram test!

Boys will be Boys

Just what is it about 'Boy's' nights out;
is it something ingrained in their heads?
Is it a hidden memory of caveman days
that now extends to their need of sheds?

Man caves, stag nights and boys nights out,
is this what men have to do to bond?
Or is it merely an all male conspiracy
and we females are just being conned.

He says, "The boy's are all going there."
He says, "The boy's they're all doing this."
But what that message actually means,
is they're all going out on the piss!

Whether it's another Sunday fishing trip
or a jolly boys outing away at the races,
they always end up one way or another
coming back smashed out of their faces.

Then he says that he's really missed me,
"Yeah right, like a hole in the head!"
Now he thinks that he's so irresistible
and his slurred words will get me to bed.

"You've got no chance Bucko," I tell him,
"I don't want to hear another peep.
The only thing you're gonna do in bed
is to sober up in a semi-dead sleep!"

Then I have to help him up the stairs,
"Just why are we attracted to men!"
Then I have to make sure that if he gets up,
....he doesn't piss in the wardrobe again!

History of my BOObs

Pancakes, fried eggs, my first bra,
lumps, bumps, too small by far.
Pert, emerging, growing well,
fuller, plumper, *bloody hell!*
Cups overflowing, another bra.
Boys are looking, I'm a star!
Jiggling, wiggling, bouncing around,
buxom beauties, *hey slow down!*

Perfectly formed handfuls of fun,
that fed and nourished my baby son.
After that, just not the same;
had their fifteen minutes of fame.
Now they seem somewhat deflated
but at least my man is still fixated.
So they've not lost all their appeal
as he still enjoys a bloody good feel!

The List

Going straight to sleep and starting to snore.
Running round stupidly when England score.
Not using the air freshener after having a poo.
Not finishing a job properly and saying "It'll do."
Leaving wet towels on the bathroom floor.
Going to the loo and not shutting the door.
Not changing your socks until I say they smell.
The same goes for skid marked undies as well.
Picking your nose and never using a tissue.
Thinking anniversaries are not that big an issue.
Leaving toenail clippings on the arm of the chair.
Never noticing the new highlights in my hair.
Thinking that the fairies wash up all the dishes.
Never listening properly to my Christmas wishes.
Always complaining when I buy more shoes,
when you spend more each year on booze.
Not leaving worktops all crumb free and clean.
Not knowing how to work the washing machine.
Not knowing where I keep the vacuum cleaner,
and finally, here's your worst misdemeanour.
Not letting me know that I'm still desired
and 'trying it on' now I'm too bloody tired!

What a Load of Boll**ks

Have you heard anything so ridiculous;
an ignorant statement that has no worth.
My man says that a whack in the knackers
is more painful than women giving birth!

He says females have built in painkillers,
so giving birth *can't* be as bad as we say,
so it must be more painful for mere men,
who feel their pain in the natural way!

Now I think that my man's rather lucky
that we have no more plans for kids,
because if we had then this stupid dad
and his 'opinions' would be on the skids.

I'd give him a couple of paracetamol,
to see if that made him any braver.
Then I'd employ a man to kick his knackers
for each minute that I was in labour!

His Head's in the Shed!

My man is so proud of his garden shed,
he says he built it with George, his friend.
But George did the build
while Tim mainly chilled
and now it's driving me round the bend.

Heavy duty racks were built into the roof,
so 'Man Wood' could be stored and saved.
Now this is just wood,
that's not really much good
and which a woman would just throw away!

But oh no, this man wood is special,
odd shaped bits that are kept 'just in case.'
"It would be better," I said,
"to keep spare noses instead,
just in case this big one falls off my face!"

He snapped "One day it will come in useful."
"Yes, you're absolutely right," I said,
"but only if we retire
our clapped out gas fire
and buy a wood burning stove instead!"

Everything has its own place in his shed,
all his man wood is kept in neat stacks.
There's damaged old planks,
and a few broken shanks,
with the longer bits kept on his racks.

And it's galling how it's so neat and tidy;
he even shows visitors round his shed.
It leads to numerous rows
because tidying the house,
never even enters his caveman head!

Scarred Stiff

My old friend Ann rang for old times sake
and we agreed to meet up for coffee and cake.
Two days later we met up in a down town cafe,
but her appearance took my breath right away.
Her face seemed all stiff, no longer free to frolic,
it didn't seem to move and looked rather robotic.
Too much Botox and lip fillers and Oh my God,
she now had the look of an unsurprised cod!

I know that sounds bitchy and I shouldn't criticize
but she looked like one of those 'Stepford Wives.' *
"I've had work done" she said, "what do you think."
"It looks........lovely," I lied, "but can you still blink?"
"Of course," she replied with blank faced enthusiasm,
totally missing my natural dark tones of sarcasm.
She waxed lyrical about all the treatments she'd had
and all the money it had cost. She must be mad!

* 'The Stepford Wives' is a feature film where a community in the USA replaces all their wives with look-alike robots!

Mind you, I couldn't stop gazing at her huge new bust,
wondering what they'd look like free and un-trussed.
But they were just too big and so out of proportion,
if I ever get them done I'll proceed with caution.
I'd bet her man has stretch marks round his mouth,
then she said she'd been *'tightened'* a bit further south!
She said her man was well off and had paid for it all,
so she'd booked herself in for a complete overhaul!

But then to end up with lips so disfigured and thick,
you'd think she'd been hit in the mouth with a brick!
As we parted she gave me the card for her clinic
but I hadn't been convinced being ever the cynic.
There'll be no Botox for me, no Stepford Wives,
I'll stick to my mud pack and cucumber eyes.
I'll never have that treatment and my face destroyed,
unlike my friend Ann ......who I now call Ann Droid!

Sitting Bull

My man disappeared into his shed one day;
there was a lot of banging and clattering.
"What the Hell?" I never heard myself say
as the noise level rose to ear shattering.

For six solid hours he was locked in his shed.
Had something gone awry with our marriage?
He never even bothered coming out to be fed,
and missed out on a thick sausage sandwich!

He finally came out looking pleased as punch;
he thought it was obviously quite a big deal.
Nothing would normally make him skip lunch
and now he was ready for the big reveal.

Then he pulled this *'thing'* from out the shed,
smiling like the cat that had got the cream.
"I designed it and built it myself," he said.
The strangest chair that you've ever seen!

It's seat was created from an old dartboard
and battered cricket bats formed four legs.
He'd created it all from his sporting hoard
and the backrest was an old wooden sledge.

The end of each armrest had ping pong bats,
"They're like little tables," he said with cheer.
Cut up cue's were used as strengthening laths
so they could take the full weight of a beer!

"We should think of a suitable name for it,"
he turned round to me and seriously said.
The first word that came to mind was 'Shit,'
then the word 'Bonfire' popped into my head.

'The Sporting Seat' and 'The Athletes Chair,'
came up amongst plenty of other naff names.
Now he's proudly plonked it on the patio there
and he's called it .... "Throne of Games"

Times They are a Changing

Global warming is obviously happening;
it must be happening here and now
or everyone has left their heating on,
so please soothe my fevered brow.

And now somebody seems to be putting
their clothes in my wardrobe at night.
'Cause when I get dressed in the morning
my clothes have never been *that* tight!

And I keep forgetting some silly things,
silly things I should really remember.
Like what the hell month is it now?
Is it still August or is it September?

But other than that I just have to say,
things have really gone quite smoothly,
except everyone now seems to argue a lot,
and then say that it's *ME* that's moody!

I've just realised that my man tells lies;
I think it's totally bloody outrageous.
Why on earth didn't he ever let me know,
that the hairs on his chin were contagious!

And then just what the hell did I ever see
in things like spinach and asparagus bake,
when there's all this great stuff like vodka,
chocolate, wine and double cream cake!

Have I said that I keep forgetting things?
Some things that I should really remember.
Like just what the hell month is it now,
is it still August or is it September?

So just what the hell is happening here?
I know there's really only one likely cause.
Yes, you've guessed it and here it comes,
it's the bloody dreaded menopause!

Hold Back the River

When I cough or sneeze, I get the wee's
and the remedy is Tena Lady!
If I have to shout, it just trickles on out.
Three cheers for Tena Lady!
I clench my cheeks or my front bum leaks.
No strain for Tena Lady!
When I laugh and giggle, I tend to dribble.
No jokes on Tena Lady!
With unexpected shocks, the seal unlocks.
But I'm secure with Tena Lady!
Then if I have to run my bladder's undone
and the winner is ...... Tena Lady!

But at times I forget and my legs turn wet
if I leave my 'Lady' at home in its box.
If I'm out for a while it can be quite a trial
and I squelch home with soggy pop socks!

High Bear Nation

With all this talk of sending men to Mars
and all the plans that NASA are making,
maybe an opportunity's been overlooked
and perhaps one they should be taking.

I say we should send trained bears to Mars;
they would be great for space exploration,
for they tend to spend long months asleep
in a kind of 'suspended animation.'

They could hibernate when they blast off,
then they could wake up when they land
and surely that would be so much easier
than sending a rocket ship that's 'manned.'

But should we send brown or black bears?
Well I think that both would be alright
and to stop the 'PC' crowd complaining,
we'll include a polar bear that's white.

And maybe they could all be sponsored by a large company to prove it cares, perhaps a multi- national chocolate firm who could call them all ....Mars Bears!

Death Breath

Now here's a thing I don't understand;
my man showers and smells so fresh.
He shaves and then he cleans his teeth
and then he gargles for fresh breath.

Then in bed does things that I don't like;
I should have stopped it from the start,
because the things he likes to do the most
is snore thunderously, slaver and fart.

Thank God for marriage saving earplugs
so I get some much needed sleep as well,
but the nose clip nipped and was painful
so I get to suffer his *heinous anus smell!*

But then what the Hell happens overnight?
It's like he's just had a visit from Death!
Or maybe the dog crapped in his mouth
to leave that horrendous morning breath!

Or perhaps it's when he's in a deep sleep
and his snoring is as dreadful as ever,
a valve opens up somewhere in his body
that links his arse and mouth together!

That means sex is usually in the evening,
as in the morning it's a little tricky.
Unless I put the nipping nose clip on
and have a Whizz-Bang (That's a quickie!)

Fishing Trip

My man he disappears on fishing trips;
he swans off with our neighbour, George.
They've seemed to gel and to get on well
and a good friendship has been forged.

As they ambled over the farmers land,
with his permission to fish in his lake,
Tim paid no heed to crossing the field
and that proved a mighty mistake.

His right foot stole down a rabbit hole;
he lurched forward and with a 'splat,'
still holding his gear and his box of beer,
fell headlong into a brand new cow pat.

He really shouldn't have yelled as he fell,
an open mouth was a real bad idea.
The cow pat smote the back of his throat
and set up home next to his trachea.

George couldn't really help that much
as Tim retched and spat out the muck,
for he nearly fell while laughing like hell
at Tim's hilariously funny bad luck.

Then George saw on Tim's tainted face,
some black spots round his nose and eyes.
Tim had fallen and hit the fresh cow shit
so fast that he'd flattened some flies!

"I knew you'd come back shit faced,"
I said later as he was telling the tale,
and considering it wasn't the morning,
his 'Death Breath' was right off the scale!

"So it didn't stop you going fishing then?"
I said as he returned back late in the day.
"So did you catch anything then?" I asked.
"I bloody hope not," ....was all he'd say.

Who Said Romance is Dead

Each year when my Birthday comes round,
my man always brings me breakfast in bed.
He makes stewed tea with cold burnt soldiers
along with one very hard over boiled egg!

When we're out he will open doors for me;
Listen up, now you may find this shocking.
It's so I don't have to slow down or stop
when weighed down with all the shopping!

Once he said he'd bought me some flowers
but a few seconds before I began praising,
I noticed the 'flowers' standing on the table
were of the variety, *plain and self raising!*

Oh, he thought that was the funniest thing
but then his laughing kind of turned all sour.
As I shouted "This may just help down there,"
while covering his crotch in *'self raising'* flour!

My Man's Bottom

I must tell you about my man's bottom;
he does not actually possess an arse!
It's not an illusion, his bum's Lilliputian
and getting underpants to fit is a farce.

When I try to buy him new underwear,
I have to search through the 'Small Ads,'
to find by chance some pocket sized pants
and hope they still cover up his 'nads.'

The size that fit him is one up from 'Boys,'
they're the smallest size a man can get.
He stays in the shower for nearly an hour
just to make sure his behind gets wet!

He went to consult a Physical Therapist
to see if special exercises could help a bit.
But he was confounded and quite astounded
when he found that Tim still gave a shit!

Now the Therapist has declared it official
and has confirmed his arse is not there.
So everyone please, check all your settees
because it's normally found in a chair!

So trying to buy underpants off the shelf
proved a big waste of money and time.
Then I got an idea for his missing posterior
and now in practice it works out just fine.

I buy him 'Extra Large' and I alter the rear,
so they don't hang down all saggy and slack.
I need to buy them big for his....thingamajig
and now they fit him both FRONT and back!

Hand Finished

My man was upstairs and had been there for a while,
so I thought I'd surprise him with my stealth and guile.
On tip-toes I ascended all the stairs to the landing
and saw him sat on the bed, doing that 'man' thing!

He had his back to me not expecting any interruption
as his right hand was going more than ten to the dozen.
A box of white tissues lay beside him opened and used
so shocked I backed off and went back down confused.

Then my mind formed the kind of a cunning plan
that would humble and shame my masturbating man.
"This'll teach him," I thought as I finalised my ruse.
"It would be amusing to hear his sad and feeble excuse."

So when he finally came down and he sat in his chair,
I went back up to the bedroom to prepare the snare.
As I passed I glanced into the bedroom waste bin
and "Yes, you've guessed, those used tissues were in."

I undressed and then pulled open my lingerie draw
and put the 'sexy stuff' on that he'd liked before.
Then I put on more make up and had lips painted red
and then I draped myself sexily prone on the bed.

(I wish!)

I felt silly in net stockings and black peep-hole bra
but tonight was the night I get to play a porn star!
He'd never managed to manage it twice in one night
and now I was ready to give the bastard a fright.

"Can you come up and help me," I meekly cried out.
"I'll be up in a minute," I heard my man shout.
His face was a picture when he pushed open the door
but not the shamefaced look that I was hoping for.

He ripped off his clothes and then did a little dance
and launched himself onto me with out any pants.
He wasn't spent and useless like all the other nights,
oh no, his willy was standing right up for its rights!

A while later we were both left breathless and damp;
it was now turning dark so I turned on the lamp.
"A bit earlier," I said, "when you were up here before,
I saw you doing something but what I'm not sure."

"Oh I was polishing the candlesticks from Auntie Mabel,
the silver ones that you keep on your dressing table."
There like a rebuke for my 'below the belt' scheming,
the candlesticks stood erect ....and all freshly gleaming!

Testicles!

We once watched a porn film together
but it left me un-swayed and un-fazed.
But one thing I noticed while watching;
the men had testicles all cleanly shaved.

Now my man's unkempt nether region,
needs a good trimming without a doubt.
It looks like an untidy old hairy oasis,
with a bare pink palm tree sticking out!

"So why don't *you* do that," I mentioned.
(Mind you, I think he'd need a strimmer.)
Then a glint materialized into his eyes
and he thought he was on to a winner.

"So why don't you do it for me," he asked,
"as I find it difficult to see down there."
"Okay," I said, get your razor and foam
and your nuts will swing without hair ."

With legs apart, on the bed, on a towel,
I was knelt in front of him on the floor.
He hissed "Be careful with those scissors"
and then he shuddered right to the core.

After a trim I applied some shaving foam
and soon felt a stirring begin in his 'bits.'
Then as the razor started scraping his sac
the 'creamy fondle' just lost all it's glitz.

Before long his pubic hair had been shorn
and looked the same as those 'porn men.'
Now the absent glint returned to his eyes
and then those 'stirrings' started again.

Then suddenly he just started screaming,
he was now howling and going crackers.
He never asked me to shave him again
after slapping after shave on his knackers!

(Tee hee hee)

Holey Moley

Tim got up and drew back the curtains one morn,
to find molehills adorning his pristine back lawn.
He swore and took in a sharp intake of breath
as he mentally condemned the intruder to death.

He got dressed and went out to his wooden man shed,
vowing never to give in till the damn mole was dead.
He found an old pole that he rammed down each hole,
then he stuffed back the soil so to suffocate the mole.

He came back into the house for some tea and toast.
"That's the end of that mole," I heard my man boast.
Around an hour later he walked out the back door,
to find more molehills now than there was there before!

His face contorted in rage as he mouthed an obscenity.
"It's war," he muttered with his voice full of enmity.
Then he crept up to a molehill with stealth and guile
with his pickaxe in hand and one murderous smile.

“What are you doing,” I shouted out from the house.
Tim pointed and mouthed, “Mole” as quiet as a mouse.
Then the molehill moved and then it moved some more
and his pickaxe arced down to give the mole what for!

About ten times Tim's pickaxe smacked into the earth,
swinging it wildly and swearing for all he was worth.
Then he ran back to his shed singing “I killed the mole”
and he brought back a spade to start digging a hole.

The hole was four feet wide and nearly two foot deep
before Tim eventually considered admitting defeat.
The mole had escaped and was nowhere to be found,
so he just carried on digging more holes in the ground.

His spade smacked something solid so he gave it a poke,
that's when he hit it again and the sewer pipe broke.
Sewage gushed out and it didn't smell all that sweet
when it spilled into the hole and flowed over his feet.

"Shit," Tim exclaimed and "Yes" he was right,
he was now in the shit as well as stood in the shite!
He climbed out of the hole as I came running out.
"What the Hell have you done," I snarled with a shout.

Nearly one week on and a thousand pounds later,
he was in the front room and was reading his paper.
Snidely I said "They've made a good job of the drain,
even renewing the pipe all the way to the main.

And if you'd renewed the insurance just like I'd said,
we wouldn't now be a thousand pounds in the red."
"But on the plus side" said Tim, "its got rid of the mole
and its all been re-turfed now they've filled in the hole."

Unbelievably Tim said that he thought the worst bit,
was that his trainers still smelled of our neighbours shit!
Looking out the front window, his apathy disappeared,
as on the *front* lawn now .....another molehill appeared!

The 'Big' Question

In the past I was a bit promiscuous
and was never that proper and prim.
But I preferred the term 'adventurous'
and that's how I came to meet Tim.
He bumped into me late in a nightclub,
ten minutes before it was due to close,
along with numerous other no hopers,
all going home on their own I suppose.
He looked at me and he said "Nice arse."
Then he continued with a cheeky grin,
"The last time I saw an arse like that,
it ended up in a corned beef tin!"
"No wonder you can't get a date," I said,
"your lousy chat up lines are the dregs."
"I don't need chat up lines," he replied
"with what's hanging between my legs!"
Now my interest had been truly piqued,
"So prove it," I said back with a smile,
and I ended up taking the braggart home
where we got it on together 'big style.'

And I have to say he was telling the truth,
he did prove exceedingly well endowed.
If he wore a mask in a busy nudist camp,
I could pick him right out in the crowd!
It's true what they say about a man's feet,
small footed men they can only dream.
When I met Tim my dreams came true
as his shoe size was a 'massive' Thirteen.
Now it's hard to see him as the end result,
after more than a million years of evolution.
So did nature make him more attractive
solving the problem with a 'nice' solution?
So were our courting just passion and lust?
(where we developed some 'naughty' habits.)
How did love find time to blossom and grow
because hell, we were at it like rabbits!
But looking back I have to ask the question;
(your answers on a postcard please.)
Did I only marry because his best feature,
was nearly hanging down to his knees!

Mum's the Word

When we first married and lived together,
I thought that nothing else really mattered.
But it didn't take long
before those thoughts were gone
and my rose coloured glasses had shattered.

Why? You ask, but I bet that you know.
Well I'll tell you and here it comes.
He said that my dinners
were worse than beginners
and were not nearly as good as his Mum's!

He had no tact, no compassion at all,
I couldn't believe the things he said.
I took it mostly in silence
and at times turned to violence
when I emptied the plate on his head!

Then one night we were 'getting it on.'
I thought I'd wait until he'd 'come'.
When he said "That was great."
I just couldn't wait
and said "But not as good as your Mum!"

After that he seemed to get the point,
dinner was pleasant and not a chore.
Life once more was rosy,
and we would snuggle up cosy
but that wasn't the end of Mother in Law!

New Balls Please!

When my man starts seriously snoring,
it just has to be heard to be believed.
So anything that can put a stop to this
would leave me thankful and so relieved.

He goes through many different stages
before I eventually impart him a cuff.
He begins with big bad wolf impressions;
that's when he starts to huff and puff.

Next comes sounds like a gurgling drain,
then he moves on to the coffee machine.
Then he's roaring like an old steam train
with a motor bike coming inbetween.

While lying awake I got round to thinking,
that maybe surgery might do some good.
But the surgery plan that I'm thinking of,
is not of the kind that a surgeon would!

Men say how sensitive their testicles are
and know how easy they are to breach.
So I thought it would be a brilliant idea
if they were transplanted out of reach.

So the best place that I could think of,
where they wouldn't be so easily hurt,
is transplanted onto the small of his back
and where they'd be covered by his shirt.

Then they wouldn't be so easily harmed,
and it would make his life less galling.
It would stop him lying flat on his back
.......and would stop the bugger snoring!

Sixth Sense

My eyes have gazed upon wondrous sights,
like the pyramids and the northern lights.

My ears have heard many wondrous sounds,
including waterfalls and merry-go-rounds.

My nose has sniffed some wondrous smells,
such as baking bread and spring bluebells.

My hands have touched upon wondrous things,
the likes of newborn skin and guitar strings.

My tongue has tasted many wondrous delights,
including pink champagne and fried cod bites.

My mind's been thinking some wondrous thoughts,
like peace, proper sleep.........and the Divorce Courts!

Mother in Law

Flamin' men, they can be so annoying
and it's just one of their many flaws.
Only one other thing comes really close
and yes, that's the Mother in Laws!

Mine never thought I was good enough
for her darling little blue eyed boy.
She'd snipe and take the odd pot shot
like on a mission to kill and destroy.

So I ended up calling her 'The Sniper,'
as I was in her sights from the start.
Her bullets would hit and stir the shit
and upset our happy apple cart.

She'd even cause rows when not around,
like when Tim carved open his thumb.
Even though I rushed right over to help,
he still called for his flamin' Mum!

She would whisper poison in Tim's ear
about the way things should be done.
I'd do it my way when she was about
and I would just wind her up for fun.

She tried to tell me how to raise our kids
and said they shouldn't be doing chores.
I said, "Don't tell me how to raise my kids
when I'm still bloody bringing up yours!

I disarmed her with a few home truths;
I shot right back and I really let loose!
So now she knows there's no easy prey,
we sort of get on ....with a wary truce!

A Bit of a Bust Up

Over the years I had never been all that fussed
but now thought that I'd like to improve my bust.
Not like my friend Ann who went over the top,
her boobs were so big they looked like they'd pop.*
But over time my 'assets' went down the tubes
and then I saw this advert for 'Budget Boobs.'
From £2,000 that's what the advert had said,
so quickly I went through the sums in my head.
Instead of a Greek holiday, I found I could still,
get all inclusive boobs and half board in Rhyl!

But the advert was deceptive and still out of reach;
what the Ad really meant was *£2,000 each!*
I thought it was such a misleading way to charge,
just having one done would look like Little and Large.
As for finding a bra, I'd be at the end of my tether,
having to buy two flamin' sizes to sew them together.
So we're still going to Crete, we're still getting away,
£4,000 in the end was just too much to pay.
So I sort of decided it would be a lot better by far
to make them look bigger.... in a much smaller bra!

* See page 12

What Makes a Good Marriage?

What's all this elusive 'chemistry' about,
that most people try so hard to find.
Does something physical actually happen
or is it all just a trick of the mind?

Some people search around the world
as they try to find their perfect lover.
But 'perfection' is really hard to find
as in the end we all seem to discover.

So just what makes a "good marriage."
Well it seems certain it's not 'perfection,'
but one good thing that seems to help
is a compatible and fetching erection!

Not so large that it can actually hurt
or much too small to feel that it's 'in.'
But it's really nice to have bits that fit
when you're conjoined in original sin.

They say that a 'good marriage' is forever
and say a 'good marriage' lasts for life.
But they say that a marriage only works
if the man is shit scared of his wife!

I tend to believe that could well be true,
though I think it is still to be verified.
Because I don't think Tim's scared of me,
I 'd say he's bloody terrified!

A Close Shave

Once I shaved myself 'down there,'
I thought I'd give my man a treat.
He really didn't take to it though
and said it looked just like raw meat!

He didn't like the 'plucked chicken' look
but he still got down to say "Hello."
Then a hedgehog moved into my knickers
when all the stubble started to grow!

He said that he preferred it 'Au Natural '
without any shaving, clipping or tarting.
He said he loved it just as it was before
with that lovely centre parting!

Anniversary

My man remembered our first Anniversary!
He bought me a non stick frying pan!
But he should be commended,
at least he'd remembered
and after all, he is a man!

And the second? Yes of course he forgot,
the date slipped right out of his head.
He was going fishing with friends,
then tried to make amends
by offering to take me up to bed!

Now isn't that just how a man would think?
You have sex and that's romance!
So I put the man straight
with a well aimed plate
that flattened the rod in his pants!

So if you give men a bit of firm training,
it's amazing what discipline brings.
The next year he said
the date stuck in his head
and I got some roses and lovely earrings!

And the date was never forgotten again,
due to my vexed and angered response.
So I think the best way,
so he remembers that day
is to let him forget it ....**just once!**

The Flasher

Doctor Slater told Tim to go out walking more,
to help his bad back and to strengthen his core.
I went with him one time for an evening stroll
and down a narrow tree lined road we stole.

A car came towards us and flashed its lights;
"It must be Billy" said Tim, "old Billy Sykes,
he's just retired and bought a new car like that,
he's pulling up now look, he must want a chat."

Tim bent down and peered in the passenger door
but it wasn't his mate, old Billy Sykes that he saw.
"He must want directions," a bent over Tim said
and waited for the window to wind down instead.

When the *'other'* car that the driver had flashed
had come round parked cars and had driven past,
the stopped car pulled away and left my poor Tim
crouching on the verge looking foolish and dim.

He just looked at me blankly in a state of surprise;
I started laughing so much that I actually cried.
What the driver must've thought, having pulled over
to find a strange man staring into his Range Rover?

He'd pulled away sharply as if in a state of fright,
I shrieked "I bet he thought it was a 'dogging' site."
I pulled out a tissue to wipe the tears from my face
and thanked God my Tena Lady was safely in place!

It's a Snip

My man was at the birth of our second child
and I told him then that enough was enough.
I said if he didn't book himself in for the 'snip,'
that was the last that he'd see of my muff.

So reluctantly he actually agreed that he'd go
but complained he might not 'feel like a man.'
"Oh I won't feel like a man either," I warned,
until both his balls dropped into the can!

The night before he had to shave them bare,
they were wrinkled like the neck of a turkey.
He wouldn't let me shave his pubes this time,*
so I just waved 'bye bye' to Pinky and Perky!

I took him and dropped him at the hospital,
the next day when his appointment was due.
Then I happily left him and went off shopping
and said that I'd pick him back up at Two.

*See page 31

Then when I arrived he was waiting outside
and was stood in a most peculiar stance.
Then he grimaced and ambled up to the car
like a little kid that had shit in his pants.

He moaned non stop how his knackers hurt
and how my driving was too jerky and fast.
I don't think he noticed me picking up pace
over each and every speed bump we passed.

A week or two later he stopped his moaning,
peace descended and I have to give thanks,
for knowing that childbirth was over for me
when it was proved he was now firing blanks.

When we 'got it on,' I was so much more relaxed,
it made sex better and was not detrimental.
Now I've christened it his 'Christmas Tree' willy,
because the balls are now purely ornamental!

Am. Dram. Tim

Tim and George joined the local Am. Dram. club *
and after rehearsals they all went to the pub.
"We have to" they said, "because when you start,
buying the Director drinks can win you a part."
So they 'won' a role in the Christmas Pantomime,
a part that perfectly suited their skills combined.
Tim and George were to be the pantomime horse,
so George's wife and me got free tickets of course.

So we had front row seats for the first performance,
or as Tim called it, "The Premier" on December 12th.
George was really good playing the head of the horse
and as for Tim?......... well he just played himself!

Hot Tub

We bought one of those inflatable hot tubs;
we thought it might rekindle some flames.
So it was installed just outside on the patio
next to his eyesore 'Throne of Games.' *

The roof covering the patio seating area
gave the hot tub good weather protection.
It was in a position that wasn't overlooked
and escaped all the neighbours attention.

We'd get in it at night with a bottle of wine
and it seemed to soak away our troubles.
Inhibitions dissolved and were washed away
by the billions of exhilarating bubbles.

Then we soon got round to 'getting it on,'
but he couldn't keep his damn thing in place,
being nearly weightless he kept floating away
just like he was bonking in outer space!

* See page 14

So after a little bit of experimentation,
we found different ways of 'getting it on.'
The embers were fanned and re-ignited
and Yes! our boring old sex life was gone.

But the tub began building up problems
after we were using it for quite a while,
for maintaining it and keeping it pristine
turned out to be a bit of a messy trial.

For using it as we did, night after night,
it didn't take much to get out of kilter,
especially when his collected 'end product,'
............started clogging the bloody filter!

Blood Clots!

Men all have their willy's and foreskin,
while we women have a bud in a hood.
Both sexes allegedly have the same brain
but the male brain is so misunderstood.

When a man and woman become aroused,
for a man it's different and not the same,
because the blood to a man's swollen gland
has been siphoned away from his brain.

Now this causes the man massive problems
and you may think this is quite a bit silly,
because his blood short brain is now useless
and he's being lead by his rampant willy.

Primal instinct kicks in and takes control
and poor brainless man's just swept along.
Then he'll try it on with anything or one
that comes in range of his rearing dong.

His head overflows with a primeval urge,
an overwhelming need to push it in deep.
He'll take on a plastic inflatable woman
and will even worry non inflatable sheep!

So all men should have a blood transfusion;
I think that I'll start off a new campaign,
because if men were given a bit more blood,
there'd be enough for both willy AND brain!

Hi - Bye

Men's phone calls are boring,
I'm surprised there's no snoring
and this is just part of a man's shortfalls.
They've no sooner said 'Hi'
than they're saying 'goodbye,'
so I've named them his Hi-Bye calls.

But we women know better
than just to stick to the letter,
we have super conversational powers.
When I'm on the phone
to my best friend Joan,
sometimes it can go on for hours.......

'Hi Joan it's me, how you doing today'
'Oh hello Ellie, yeah, I'm fine, I'm okay.'
'I'm just calling to see if we can arrange to meet
for some cake, a chat and a nice cup of tea.

Oh, and by the way, have you heard about Gwen?
Her love rat of a man has gone and left her again.'
'Oh no, he only moved back in again last week.'
'I know, he's left for a tart from down the street.'
'Poor Gwen, she was a bit stupid to have him back,
if you ask me she was too quick to lay on her back.'
'Aha, and My God have you seen the state of Ann.'
'You mean her who married that millionaire man?'
'That's her, she's had so much surgery she looks unreal,
I was sat there dying to give her huge boobs a feel.'
'Yeah that's the problem with marrying a millionaire,
if you start to age and sag then they look elsewhere.'
'I suppose, but what did you think of Corrie* last night,
I new those two morons would end up in a fight.'
'Yeah I'm glad that he got a good smack on the nose
and he's been taken to hospital and he's comatose.'
'Are they writing him out, is that why they fought?'
'Probably, then someone will turn off his life support.'

* Coronation Street

'I wish Tim's life support could be turned off somehow,
you'll never guess just what he's gone and done now!'
'Don't tell me he's been arrested on a boy's night out?
Oh, not something that's put your marriage in doubt?'
'No no, in the back garden he dug a flamin' great hole
because he was trying to capture and murder a mole.
Then he only went and smashed the main sewer pipe
and it cost us nearly a grand to put the thing right!'
'Oh God, I wouldn't like to be in his shoes right now,
I bet that must have ended in a right blooming row!'
'Yeah too right, and you know, he's still in the shit,
he'd let the insurance lapse, now he's paying for it!
Anyway when we meet up just what are you wearing,
we don't want to be the same and have people staring.'
'Oh sorry Ellie, I can't make it, we're jetting away,
we've just booked a bargain last minute holiday.'
'Ooh that sounds lovely and off peak will be cheap.'
'Yeah it's a week all inclusive on the island of Crete.'

'That's where we went with my 'boob job' money!
Tim drank too much Ouzo and got a bad tummy.
Well, when I say 'tummy' I really mean a bad rear,
he spent two days rooming with Mr. Diarrhoea!
'TWO DAYS! you can get tablets now that stop it dead.'
'I know, I said it was that but gave him aspirin instead!
Well, he was getting drunk on Ouzo and acting the fool,
so I got two peaceful days lazing round a nice pool.'
'Oh Ellie, I never thought you could be such a swine
but I'll keep that in mind for that husband of mine!'
'Ha ha, well have a nice time and get lovely and brown,
now I'll go and watch Corrie while he's not around.
See you soon then, give me a ring when you're back
and we'll meet up and have a nice little chat.
Bye bye'
'Okay, bye Ellie.'

Tim's phone call............
'Hi,
George its Tim, the pub about 8?'
'Yeah no problem, see you there mate.'
'Bye.'

A Hard Pill to Take

My man came home from the pub one night
and what I saw made my heart stand still.
For there in his hand was the latest thing,
a sex life enhancing Viagra pill.

And I have to say that I was really intrigued
as to what the 'end' results would actually be.
So he took it and waited nearly half an hour,
before shouting down he was ready for me.

I went up to the bedroom not expecting much
but I have to say that I was genuinely amazed.
He was naked on the bed and *really* aroused
just like we were back in our courting days!

"Just look at this," he said and look I did,
I'd never seen 'this' so firm and hard.
If his body was the City of London
then 'this' was stuck up like the 'Shard.'

I felt his heart a pounding like never before;
I felt it hammering while laid on my back.
After a while I became somewhat concerned
that it might be the start of a heart attack!

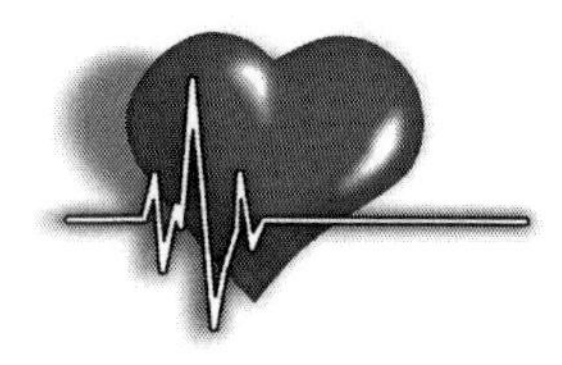

Blood vessels had burst in both of his eyes
and they were beginning to turn a bit red.
It was like being bonked by the Semen Demon
and I was convinced that he'd soon be dead.

So I stretched out my arm across the bed
and disguised it with a long sultry moan.
But what I was actually trying to figure out,
was if I could still reach the bedside phone!

If he died he would have been a 'dead' weight
and he would have pinned me to the bed,
now the consequences of something like that
are normally far better off left unsaid.

Next morning he came down for breakfast
and he was wanting to know my thoughts.
I said the tablet was far too strong for him
as it was still pushing out of his shorts.

"Next time," he said, "I'll take half a tablet,"
"Next time my arse!" I said in a flash.
"Alright," he replied with a glint in his eye,
..........."I guess I'd give that a bash!"

A Run of Noses

My nose it grows like a big red rose,
flowering on my face.
And when it runs
my nose becomes
a rose with the stalk in place!

A green river flows down my nose.
It's such a poorly designed face.
So why didn't God,
the silly old sod
put my mouth in a different place!

I seem to have quite a sizeable nose,
it's maybe as big as you can get.
Taking a shower's a trial,
as I look up for a while
to make sure that my boobs get wet!

Two noses they had an argument;
these noses they were foes.
If one hadn't run,
(please pardon the pun)
I'm sure it would have come to blows!

The most useful noses I supposes
are those that belong to Eskimoses.
In frozen lands
they don't shake hands
but rub noses to say their Hello'ses.

So why did I end up with a nose like this,
it's big and red and chunky.
This nose would be handsome,
good looking and then some,
if it was owned by a proboscis monkey!

Sex Darling?

I find it alarming when my man calls me 'Darling,'
because I know his mind is thinking about nookie.
But the odds that he will have his way with me
would be about a hundred to one with a bookie.

It's not that I'm tired but I just can't get inspired,
why he calls me 'Darling' has become quite clear.
It's after a few rounds down the Fox and Hounds
and he's now sozzled after a skin full of beer.

At first it was charming, I liked being called 'Darling,'
It seemed romantic and it made my heart throb.
But then the drink took effect and only semi erect
.............the drunken bugger fell asleep on the job!

Tena Man

I've found that in these terribly P.C. times,
some companies still commit P.C. crimes.
For example the firm that makes 'Tena Lady,'
doesn't seem approach the subject humanely.
'Cos if you ask me they've got a flamin' cheek,
as it infers that it's only us ladies that leak.
I think they may be actually missing a trick
or those running the company aren't very slick.

A golden opportunity is there just ready to take.
A rich vein has been missed with money to make.
If they brought out a "Tena Man" product at last,
skid marks in pants would be a thing of the past!
My laundry basket can't be good for my health,
when it smells like a wet dog that's shit itself.
So come on and get 'Tena Man' out in a hurry
and save us from the fallout of an Indian curry!

Enter the Dragon

I remember the first time that we 'got it on.'
I remember the date, the time, and the place.
I thought Tim was quite an attractive man,
..........*until he revealed his hideous 'cum face.'*

For those first few seconds, hell he was ugly
as his face shuddered and juddered away.
I couldn't believe how his features all changed
and it's still haunting me right to this day.

It reminded me of that film 'Enter the Dragon,'
you know, the Kung Fu movie starring Bruce Lee.
Where he fights and pulls those screwed up faces;
well that's exactly what he looked like to me.

When that moment 'comes' I now close my eyes
and imagine George Clooney has taken his place.
But Enter the Dragon still seeps into my mind,
so now I've christened it ....his 'Cum Fu face!'

A Hairy Situation

On women pubic hair is perplexing,
just why do we grow it down there?
It makes no sense growing hair so dense,
when it might be better off bare?

But I suppose it did help primitive man,
when the 'prize' was a little bit hairier.
At least he knew it would give him a clue
that he was splodging in the right area.

So it's bad enough to have a hidden muff
but veiling the bud was a massive mistake.
Hiding it within even more folds of skin
caused the orgasms we've all had to fake!

So just why do women have pubic hair?
I think someone has made a big bungle.
The not so clever don't find buried pleasure
while fighting their way through a jungle!

Bedroom Action

I was tidying in our bedroom,
I was hoovering under the bed.
Then I shouted "My dear,
why don't you come in here
and I'll give you a little head."

Tim trotted into the bedroom,
erotic thoughts filling his head.
Before he had a chance
to drop his pants,
his erotic thoughts dropped dead.

I was sitting laughing on the bed
and waved "bye" to his semi-erection.
For there on the bed,
was the long lost head
from his Action Man collection!

The following poem concerns a subject that every woman does, or has complained about in the past or will in the future. But complaining never makes any difference and here are some of the excuses why!.

Angle of the Dangle

He just pissed and he just missed the toilet,
yes there's wee once more on the floor.
He says he holds it at the right angle
and he doesn't just let it dangle
but it squirts in all directions
like his knob's been through a mangle!

And after sex he says he gets
a peculiar double stream jet,
where one I think, hits the sink
and the other leaves his legs wet.
Like every other man he misses the can,
yes there's wee once more on the floor.
He aims to please but then when he pee's
it sprinkles on the floor like before.

He says if women had to aim
the results would be the same,
so down we squat to hit the pot
so we women can still complain!
He says he takes care but it's so unfair,
yes there's wee once more on the floor.
He leaves a mess, his aim is a guess,
I need to find a cure that's for sure!

Now this is his very last warning
and yet he stands there yawning,
thinking "She's asleep, if I leave it to steep,
it will all be dry by morning!"
When he uses the loo his aims not true,
yes there's wee once more on the floor.
It gathers and flows around his bare toes
Then moving makes him miss it even more!

Then he paddles out of the puddle
and crosses the landing at the double.
Now his feet are cold so he grabs hold
and tries to give me a cuddle!
He aims for the middle but with wayward piddle,
yes there's wee once more on the floor.
So to solve this puzzle, I make him piss in a funnel,
and now he never misses anymore!!

But he says he holds it at the right angle
and that he doesn't just let it dangle
but it squirts in all directions,
like his knob's been through a mangle!

A Careless Whisker

My man once grew himself a beard;
I never liked the look of it at all.
It was even worse than I first feared
and he looked like a right oddball.

It was far too straggly and tickled,
you know, when we'd 'get it on.'
In dainty places it just bloody prickled
and yes, I soon wished it was gone.

He looked just like an evil hypnotist
and his appeal now left me yawning.
So his hirsute face was left unkissed
and I gave him this stern warning.

"You shave it off right now," I said,
"you know you look a bloody mess."
But what was his response instead?
I'm pretty sure that you can guess.

His bloody beard grew even longer,
his bloody beard grew ever thicker.
But my resolve grew even stronger
and I gave a wide birth to his zipper.

After two weeks he started pleading,
saying that we still should 'get it on'.
I said there's no way I'm conceding
until those whiskers have all gone.

Then a few days later when I came in,
I found some roses of the deepest red.
He bellowed "My beard is in the bin,
...............and I'm upstairs on the bed!"

Re-incarnation

If my man was ever re-incarnated
I think he might come back as a snail,
he doesn't move fast and lives to eat
and always leaves one messy trail.

Then again he could return as a sheep,
as he just follows all of his mates.
His star sign is actually Aries the Ram,
so just who knows what fate awaits?

Or perhaps he'll return as a donkey!
Now I don't have to explain that do I?
Or maybe he'll take the form of a snake;
a large pink one with only one eye!

But then again and knowing his luck,
he'll come back as a man again next life
and find another muggins to do it all,
another fool, a numpty ....a *wife!*

A Growing Problem

Just what's going on with my hair 'down there,'
it now grows like its owned by a Grizzly bear!
Before it seemed to keep itself lovely and neat
but now needs shearing more often than sheep.
My man's noticed that I trim it more than before,
saying he finds 'dead muffs' on the bathroom floor!

He calls it my 'Were-Muff,' saying it starts to bloom
and grows hairier each time we have a full moon!
So those bikini waxes, well I've just had to shun,
she emptied the wax pot and I was only half done!
In the end she said she had to charge me double,
then 'itchy muff' syndrome arrives with the stubble!

It's not as lush as before, it's now wiry and drier,
just one stray spark and it could start a bushfire!
But I can't give up now that the battles begun,
I think I need to go get me a sandblasting gun!
It's getting worse now, much worse than I feared,
now my man understands why I hated his beard!

What a Rip Off

When Tim had his chest waxed for charity,
his skin looked sore and red like a devil
and as for the pain that he couldn't take,
he took screaming to a different level.

But I have to say I quite enjoyed his pain
after what he'd said about us giving birth.*
I even got to slowly rip off a wax strip,
making sure I got my 50p's worth!

I couldn't believe how loud Tim screamed,
then again, his chest was a real hairy place.
His face screwed up in pain and shuddered
and looked exactly like his 'Cum Fu' face! **

He thought they'd ripped his nipples off,
mind you, there was a trickling of blood.
That was when he only went and fainted
and hit the floor with a sickening thud.

* See page 9
**See page 71

He'd fallen forward right onto his face
and I thought he'd maybe broken his nose.
His two front teeth had been dislodged
and he was unconscious and comatose.

The ambulance arrived to take him away;
"What the Hell's happened here," they said.
They couldn't tell if he was beaten or burned
with his 'medium rare' skin and bloody head!

After a week off work and a big dental bill,
he no longer looked like he'd been in the wars
and I'm quite sure that the £9.50 he raised
was given to a genuinely worthwhile cause!

Chastity?

A long way back in time, back in the days of yore,
armoured knights rode off to their crusades and war.
Leaving their ladies at home in their halls and castles,
they needed a way to keep out other medieval tassels.
So local blacksmiths were sought and then were hired
to make steel belts in which their maids were attired.

So while away for years on their 'jolly boys' crusade,
do you think their maids all 'honoured and obeyed?'
Although the chastity belts remained secure and locked,
the knights would be dismayed, disgusted and shocked,
to find their maids found ways of getting some nookie
and some were living it up and were making whoopee.

When 'the boys' returned from their 'bonding' crusades,
they immediately *'wanted'* their fair and chaste maids.
One found his lady in the forge, knelt on the bellows,
in front of two of the belt making blacksmith fellows.
The knight got a consummate vision of medieval porn
and as she knelt on the bellows, *the 'blow job' was born!*

Bar Stool Fool

Is there anything you've done
that has left you stunned,
something really stupid and naff.
Well a situation occurred
because of crossed words
and I made one hell of a gaffe.

Our old kitchen was tired
so a new one was acquired,
with a new breakfast bar attached.
Then we ran round like fools
trying to find some bar stools,
the right colour and style that matched.

We looked high and low
and what do you know,
we eventually found them in MFI.
The only thing they lacked
was they came flat packed,
so I attempted my first DIY.

I was quick off the blocks
and took them out of the box
and then tried to put them together.
I used an old pair of pliers
and two kinds of screwdrivers
but it still seemed to take me forever.

With a smile on my face
I put the stools into place,
they were the final and finishing piece.
They'd been long on my mind
as it was so hard to find
bar stools the right shade of cerise.

Then just one day later
I went to see Dr. Slater,
who's quite severe and can't abide fools.
At the end of the appointment
he prescribed me some ointment
and then he said "How are your stools."

I thought, "Who told him?
Has he been talking to Tim?"
It just never 'clicked' whatsoever.
I said "They're a nice cerise shade,
really solid and well made,
but they took ages to put together!"

I saw the look on his face
as I shut the door in its place
and then I realised just what I'd said.
Now because of my stools
I'd become one of his 'fools.'
and now see a different Doctor instead!

Bedroom Gardening

My man likes his garden and he keeps it real neat,
he mows it and mulches the plants with good peat.
But if you ask me I think that he mows it too much
but he insists he possesses that 'green fingered' touch.
He splits clumps of plants that are growing real well,
with a spade and he finds them a new place to dwell.
So normally it's all orderly and kept under control,
except for the time he went to war with '*that mole.*'
Then one night we were engaged in 'getting it on,'
but he just kept on giggling till the passion was gone.

I snapped "Just what the hell has got into your head."
"I've thought of a funny new name for sex," he said.
"Be careful" I replied, "I'm already losing the mood,"
as I new it would be 'laddish' and most probably rude.
Then he said something so bad, it gave me the hump.
The name he came up with.....was 'Splitting the Clump!'
Then he complained when I turned over to go to sleep,
I said "Well you shouldn't be so unromantic and cheap."
Now when he's in the mood and he feels a 'hardening,'
he enquires if I'm up for some *'bedroom gardening!'*

Rumour Has It

Now apparently rumour has it,
that there's a rumour going round
and it's rumoured that this rumour
has spread right across the town.

Do you know how rumours start?
and how hard they are to undo?
As it's rumoured that this rumour,
is all about '*that man*' and you!

The 'vicious rumours' are hard to kill,
for they rarely die on they're own.
Rumours should be killed when young,
instead of facing them fully grown.

The 'nasty' rumour feeds and grows,
so full of lies and sweet deceit.
Now friends all wonder if you are
shagging '*that man*' across the street!

At times the rumour lies dormant
and it can spread itself no longer,
until resurrected with the kiss of life
by the mysterious 'rumourmonger'.

So how do rumours come to life?
From some malicious lie or myth?
But what goes round comes around
and it can hit you back forthwith.

The rumourmongers are shady figures,
taking great pleasure in their labours
and rumour has it that a rumourmonger
lives next door to your neighbours!

A Phoney Letter

Years ago to communicate, you had to write a letter,
now even after all this time it hasn't got much better.
Phones were invented and they became quite cheap
and then instead of writing you were able to speak.
It was great, it was brilliant, what a revelation,
all those letters were replaced with conversation.

Then phones became mobile; they were on the move
and technology raced on and began to improve.
Then along came texting, the latest sensation,
putting an end to now normal phone conversation.
Now with Twitter and Facebook it hasn't got better,
so give me your hash tag ... and I'll write you a letter!

A Bitch in Time

Sometimes I wonder how we're still together
with what I've had to put up with 'him.'
But then when I actually sit down and think,
it must have been quite a lot worse for Tim!

No wonder he went to the pub so much,
he did it to distance himself from me,
when brain fog and the red mist descended
and I was consumed with dread PMT.

Those jolly boys outings and weekend trips,
they never randomly came out of the blue.
I realise now they'd been perfectly timed
to coincide with the days before I was due!

Sometimes I could be totally unreasonable
while suffering from the effects of PMT.
He said he'd rather negotiate with terrorists
than try to talk and reason with me!

And even when he'd done nothing wrong,
I could become a completely evil bitch.
I'd wash his pants in powder he reacted to,
just to make sure his privates would itch!

Me, the completely evil bitch

Now things have got much better without,
all the brain fog and those red mist rushes,
but why did they both have to be replaced
with all these bloody red hot flushes!

Bloody Hell!

Bloody Hell! The bus is coming,
I can see it rolling up the road.
So I start to trot towards the stop
my face set with a grim forebode.

Bloody Hell! The bus is quicker
than these little legs can run.
The odds of me catching the No. 3
have just increased to ten to one.

Bloody Hell! The bus has passed me
and it's now pulling into the stop.
The extra pounds are weighing me down,
thanks to our local pizza shop.

Bloody Hell! I'm going to make it!
The passengers they begin to cheer.
Then to my dismay the bus pulls away
as kids laugh at me from the rear.

Bloody Hell! I must look ridiculous,
Bloody Hell! Now I'm starting to cuss.
Then I run on past going extra fast,
pretending I never wanted the bus!

Bloody Hell! I shouldn't run like that,
it's made me dribble out some wee.
Because I was late, I made a mistake.
and forgot to add my Tena Lady!

Bloody Hell! I can actually feel it;
it's running down my panty hose.
As I'm shopping my legs'll be sopping
and I'll end up with wet 'pissy toes!'

A Tail of Two Dickies

I know you may think this sounds rather silly
but I've given a pet name to my man's willy.
Sorry, what I really mean is *two* names in fact
and I apologise beforehand for my lack of tact.
Like all other willy's, his has a split personality
that comes to the fore with a great regularity,
and you never know which one is on the roster,
the weak little wimp *or the big trouser monster!*
One is flaccid and placid and has little attraction,
while its wicked big twin comes out ready for action!
He's harder and aggressive, far bulkier and chunky
and screams in Tim's head, *"**DUNK ME, DUNK ME!**"*
Sometimes he appears and rears up his red head,
in the morning when my man is asleep in his bed.
That's when I get up and go quietly downstairs
before he wakes and asks me to sample his wares!
His 'morning breath' is awful as I've mentioned before,
I'm pretty sure it could be used in a biological war!
Oh sorry, yes, I was saying, they've both got a name
and maybe you've heard of their celebrity and fame.
One's soft and gentle, the other hard and cock-eyed,
So I call softy Dr. Jekyll ....and the other Mr. Hyde!

Wind of Change

Why have I now started farting?
It's something I never used to impart.
We would eat the same food
and I don't mean to be rude
but it was always him who would fart.

If we had both eaten beans on toast,
an hour later he'd start to boff.
But with me he found
there was never a sound,
he used to think I siphoned it off!

But now, my God I'm catching up
and it's not just a whiffy breeze.
I don't mean to be coarse
but it's hurricane force
.......especially when I sneeze!

It always catches him un-awares;
I never give a warning shout.
He just hears a rumbling,
akin to dull thundering
as my buttock lifts to let it out.

It always seemed worse on Sundays,
especially when Mother in Law came.
Sometimes those greens
can be worse than baked beans
and thank God for the dog to blame!

So just what the hell has happened?
I can't complain about 'him' again!
I went through 'the change,'
and it's really quite strange
'cos now.........we both fart like men!

The Fall Girl

Yesterday I fell over while walking in the street
and straight away jumped back onto my feet.
I walked on ungainly trying to hide my limp,
trying hard not to look like the proverbial 'gimp.'
Had anyone noticed me take the street tumble?
I pretended to smile but I just wanted to grumble.

My new leggings were torn and tainted with dirt
but I walked on pretending it didn't really hurt.
There was a lump on my knee the size of an egg
and I'm sure there was blood running down my leg.
But I couldn't stop there to check on the trauma,
I walked bravely on ....till I turned round a corner!

Only then could I halt and examine the damage
that the tumble had caused to my undercarriage.
Yes, blood was running from the cuts to my skin
and my new torn leggings were now for the bin.
But it was my own fault really, I shouldn't moan,
I should look where I'm going, *not at my phone!*

Foreplay

Most women would like more foreplay,
where they kiss and embrace and caress.
But men instantly want to just get it on;
and for foreplay they couldn't care less!

Once a man is aroused and in the mood,
his willy's like a Sat Nav nookie finder.
His head just tells him to clamber right on,
or even better, to ride from behind her.

To most women foreplay is a subtle art,
though for most men it's a piece of cake.
For my man's idea of romantic foreplay
is "Darling................are you still awake?"

Woo is Me

At the start men must pretend to be considerate,
never revealing or betraying their true inner idiot.
They woo us and behave when on a romantic date
and we never seem to realise until it's far too late.

Those wet farts, skidmarks and dribbled in pants,
never appear at the start of a budding romance.
Then it's all flowers and sweet nothings in your ear
until you're on 'farting terms,' ......then they appear.

'Farting Terms' as I call it, is when you both start,
not leaving the room when you push out a fart.
But by then it's too late and you're in far too deep
and you've realised he snores once he's fallen asleep.

We'd take romantic walks and have cosy nights in,
now I sit and watch the slaver dribble down his chin,
as he lays snoring in his 'watching the telly' chair
and leaves me sitting by myself playing 'solitaire.'

That's when I playback the recording of our wedding
and notice all the pounds that I should be shedding.
Then I rewind it to see myself back down the aisle,
leaving him at the altar .....and that makes me smile!

A Lean Year

I had piled on the pounds over Christmas
and thought, "My God I'm turning to flab."
Where I used to be able to 'pinch an inch '
has slowly transformed into 'grab a slab!'

Maybe it's just that I'm now getting older
and my body no longer feels the need.
Maybe now it's just settling for comfort
and has give up on the need for speed.

But then I heard of a new type of diet;
it was radical, called 'Shag Yourself Slim.'
You do it twice a day for a about a year
but did that put the pressure on Tim!

"TWICE A DAY FOR A YEAR!" Tim exclaimed.
He thought that I was being wildly deluded.
But he changed his mind when he realised
that a years supply of Viagra was included.

This time he took just one half a tablet*
and it worked just like it should oughta.
Except for once when we went swimming
and he had to stay in the bloody water!

For the next year we did it twice a day
and now I look so streamlined and slim.
But that can't be said of the grey old man
who last year was my once a week Tim!

* See page 64

Too Much to Ask?

Am I just asking too much, is it too much to ask?
To want a man who's handy and can multi-task!
I know it sounds like I'm asking for rather a lot
from a man who's magnificent at diddly-squat.

I should have recognised the signs of things to come
when he found it hard to walk while chewing gum!
We women normally juggle several balls in the air,
making breakfast, dressing kids and doing our hair!

But no, men can only manage one thing at a time,
asking them to do more is like committing a crime.
Just give them one job and they're happier by far,
like sending them to buy drinks at a crowded bar!

What do you think would happen in all probability
if men were blessed with our multi tasking ability.
Would it make our world easier and a better place
or spawn even more problems for women to face?

It's bad enough now but then at least we still cope,
so maybe 'multi-task man' would be a slippery slope.
They're quite easy to influence and easier to control
in their *"I've only got one bloody pair of hands"* role.

So on second thoughts it might be just better by far
to leave these mono-task men as they actually are,
because men are so basic and are not that complex;
........they can't even talk when they're having sex!

Muffs

Apparently there are many types of vagina,
like Ms. Barbie, where it's neat and contained.
It's the prettiest type
that's normally quite tight
and always keeps Ken entertained!

Then along comes our little Ms. Tulip;
a delightful entranceway to the womb.
She looks I think,
like a flower of pink
always appearing just ready to bloom.

Then Ms. Horseshoe canters into the frame,
she spreads wider at the top of course.
Now back in the day,
old wives would say
that their mother had been kicked by a horse!

Ms. Puffymuff is next and is still quite neat
but looks bloated and more puffed out.
It's a much a softer entry
and its quite elementary,
I wish mine was like that without doubt.

Then comes a type called Ms. Curtains,
she's quite laid back and likes to hang out.
Her lips hang low
and what do you know,
in a wind they start flapping about.

Mine sort of falls into this classification
but goes quite a bit further than that.
My man once said
that if I sat on his head,
I could be a hat with a built in chin strap!

Well Well Well

It seems quite peculiar when our men are ill,
that these 'tough macho' guys soon go downhill.
All it takes is for them to have an aching head
and away they go moaning to lie down in bed.

But do they lie in silence? Oh no that's absurd,
his moans get louder to make sure I've heard!
"I'm dying" he says, "my lips have gone blue."
"No they haven't," says I, "it's just man flu."

"No it's not!" he complains for all he's worth,
"you've got built in painkillers for giving birth,
so you women never know just how bad it is,
and stand there laughing and taking the piss!"

He can't believe that I think it's all just a con
and he says I'll be sorry when he's finally gone.
Then next thing he's gone, he was right after all;
he's gone down town on a stag night pub crawl!

The Barbecue

What happens to men when the sun comes out?
What kind of metamorphosis then takes place?
"Lets have a barbie," you'll hear them all shout,
and cooking alfresco they all seem to embrace!

It's like a throwback to caveman hunting trips,
where they'd cook their prey on an open fire.
But now it's about as rare as a total eclipse
and only when temperatures get a bit higher.

So I tried turning the central heating up high
to see if it clicked the 'cook' switch in his head.
But all it did was make him perspire and sigh
and then off he went to cool down in his shed!

So you'll hardly ever see Tim in the kitchen
even though I've tried hard to get him to cook.
After all these years of my cussin' and bitchin'
in the kitchen he couldn't give a *damn.*

So we have a barbie and we invite our friends,
Tim puts the coals on and sets them alight.
But for me it seems like the work never ends
and then he wonders why I'm getting uptight.

I do all the shopping, then marinate the meat;
I prepare all the salad, the sauces and rice,
the buns are to butter, the chicken to preheat
and Tim's drinking beer ....*"That's nice"*

Then he 'cooks' the burgers and infused meat,
and he does them, as he calls it, *'well done.'*
I check to see everyone has a drink and a seat
........and then get sent a solitary sausage bun!

I go round with a bin bag collecting the waste;
the number of beer cans is quite alarming.
My man is now well on his way to 'shit faced'
and will soon start calling me "Darling!"

At the close of the barbie I can't believe my ears
as the guests are all leaving full and replete.
Everyone's saying "Great barbie Tim, cheers."
.....and all ***he*** *did was burn the meat!*

'Sounds Like' Charades

At Christmas we played a game of family charades;
Tim had to mime the song *'Mockingbird Hill.'*
And as these things do, the mimes turned a bit blue
as Tim mimed 'Mock' with great 'sounds like' skill.

He was holding his hand round an imaginary gland
and he made it much bigger like most men will.
It's hard to believe this but my sister yelled "Penis"
and our son guessed it was Penis-ingbird Hill!

As the wine started to flow, Tim then had to 'go,'
saying "Please excuse me, but I'll just be a tick."
Then when he pulled up his fly Tim let out a cry;
as the too quick zipper ripped into his dick!

With his manhood in the zip, Tim bit on his lip
as he endured the worst pain that he'd ever felt.
He started to curse but each move made it worse
as he was trying carefully to unbuckle his belt.

With tears in his eyes, blood dripped to his thighs
as the zipper cut into the soft skin like a knife.
He was stuck in the loo not knowing what to do,
and finally started shouting for me, his wife.

I managed to unshackle his now mangled tackle
and then I tried wrapping it up in a bandage.
As I fiddled 'it' bled and reared its ugly red head
and the dressing fell off his wounded appendage.

I tried many a way to get the dressing to stay
but I wasn't a qualified or bona fide 'bone setter.'
So I felt a bit silly trying to wrap up Tim's willy
and he seemed happier when I just kissed it better!

Now the trousers Tim buys all have button up flies,
"I'm never going through that again," he squealed.
Now a month on from that day, I'd like to convey,
that the scars on Tim's "Mock" have all healed!

This poem was inspired by my wonderful mother, who in her later years developed the dreaded Alzheimer's disease. Although it is a tragically debilitating condition, looking back it did cause some truly comedic moments that will stay fondly with me as part of my memories of a fantastic lady.

My Mother's Christmas

Snow is laying,
relatives staying.
Strange faces
from stranger places.

"What was his name?
Where was he from?
Am I going daft?
Has my memory gone?"

Don't just sit there
quiet as a mouse,
"Mum, you're sitting
in the wrong bloody house!"

What I Want

(and what I've got)

A rambling house with rooms yet to be discovered.
(A three bedroom semi with an understairs cupboard.)

An expensive sporty red car with a roof 'cabriolet.'
(An old second hand Citroen in gun metal grey.)

A boob job, liposuction and new dental veneers.
(Saggy tits, weight problems and dentistry fears.)

All household chores to be done by topless au pairs!

(A plug in hoover with bag under the stairs.)

Wined and dined in restaurants serving 'Michelin' grub.
(Half a lager and a cheeseburger down at the pub.)

Designer clothes that tend to flatter my figure.
(Clothes hiding my flab another size bigger.)

Exotic holidays that includes a penthouse suite.
(Saving up for ages for two weeks in Crete.)

Fabulously good sex with foreplay delights.
(A bit of a whizz-bang on Saturday nights.)

Separate bedrooms would just be ideal for me.
(If his snoring is too bad I sleep on the settee.)

A circle of posh friends (but would they talk about me?)
(Fun hard working friends who meet up for coffee.)

A rich handsome man (but they tend to 'play away.')
(A man who still loves me in his own special way.)

Spoilt brats getting 'old school' business degrees.
(Polite children who say 'Thank you' and 'Please.')

A man who would do anything for his grumpy old wife.
(The same as above .... it's not such a bad life!)

Outroduction

Thank you for putting up with my raves and rants
about my flamin' man and his lack of romance .
If you've seen shades of *your* man, I have to say,
they may look different but all have the same way.
He will always desire his night out with the boys
and will always like playing with his big boys toys.
He's not interested at all in Rom-com chick flicks
unless the buxom leading lady likes flashing her bits.
He may not understand why you like a good read
and when you say it's a good book, he pays no heed.
But there is one book that he might read one day;
it's a book that's entitled ....'Fifty Sheds of Grey!' *

Ellie Kelly

* Actually available on Amazon!

25909114R00068

Printed in Great Britain
by Amazon